STOP PROCRASTINATING

AND TAKE BACK CONTROL OF YOUR LIFE

RUTH BARRINGHAM

ISBN: Paperback: 978-0-6454502-6-2
          eBook   978-0-6454502-7-9

Book cover image courtesy of passionart/stock.adobe.com

Disclaimer:

The Author and Publisher have used their best efforts in preparing this book. The Author and Publisher make no representation or warranties with respect to the accuracy, applicability, fitness, or completeness of the contents of this book.

The information contained in this book is strictly for information purposes. Therefore, if you wish to apply ideas contained in this book, you are taking full responsibility for your actions. Whilst we hope you find the contents of this book interesting and informative; the contents are for general information purposes only and do not constitute advice. We believe the contents to be true and accurate as at the date of writing but can give no assurances or warranty regarding the accuracy, currency, or applicability of any of the contents in relation to specific situations and particular circumstances.

This book is not intended to be a source for advice, and thus the reader should not rely on any information provided in this book as such. Readers should always seek the advice of an appropriately qualified person in the reader's home jurisdiction. The Author and Publisher of this book assume no responsibility for information contained in this book and disclaim all liability in respect of such information. In addition, none of the content of this book will form any part of any contract or constitute an offer of any kind.

Any links to third party websites are provided solely for the purpose of your convenience. Links made to websites are made at your own risk and the Author and Publisher accept no liability for any linked sites. When you access a website, please understand that it is independent from the Author and Publisher and the Author and Publisher have no control over the content of that website.

Further, a link contained in this book does not mean that the Author or Publisher endorses or accepts any responsibility for the content or the use of such website. The Author and Publisher do not give any representation regarding the quality, safety, suitability, or reliability of any of them or any of the material contained within them. Users must take their own precautions to ensure that what is selected for use is free of such items as viruses, worms, trojan horses and other items of a destructive nature.

All websites, products and services are mentioned, without warranty of any kind, either express or implied, including, but not limited to, the implied warranties of merchant ability and fitness for a particular purpose.

Table of Contents

"We all have a will to fail. It's subconscious... It's human nature. We almost always act in order to avoid pain. So rather than try something and possibly fail, we freeze up. Or we choose something easy because we know there's no risk of failure. We don't act boldly.

"Our job is to fight that will to fail, to give it the boot."

~ **James Scott Bell**
How to Write Pulp Fiction

Stop Procrastinating
And Take Back Control of Your Life

Why Do We Procrastinate?

No one really knows why we procrastinate, not even ourselves, yet we all do it all the time.

Strangely enough, it's not just the unpleasant things that we procrastinate about, but also the things we say we enjoy doing.

How often have you said you're going to do something like go for a day out, or go to the cinema, or spend time doing something else you enjoy, only to change your mind at the last minute and binge watch TV instead?

And we do the same with important things we need to do.

As a writer, I often find myself reluctant to sit down and write even though writing is something I enjoy doing. Some days I'll even think a pile of ironing looks more interesting than the writing I have to do.

No matter what it is, we all procrastinate in our own way for reasons we don't understand, and probably never will.

According to studies that have been done on this subject, there are three reasons why we procrastinate.

1. **Fear.** We fear criticism, failure, and starting something. It's easy to understand being afraid of criticism and failure, yet it's starting that most of us fear.

13

2. **Laziness**. Doing something new is hard. It takes us out of our comfort zone. Not doing something is so much easier than doing something.

3. **Lack of Interest**. We don't know how to do something until we start, so have no interest in starting something new, nor in learning the process of doing it. We just can't be bothered to even think about it.

What is Procrastination?

To procrastinate means to put off, delay, or postpone doing something.

It comes from the16th Century Latin word, "procrastinat" which means "deferred till morning."

This comes from the verb "procrastinare" with 'pro' meaning 'forward' and 'crastinus' meaning 'belonging to tomorrow (from 'cras' tomorrow).

The word "procrastinate" is similar to the word "prevaricate" meaning to speak or act in an evasive way, in much the way politicians do when speaking with journalists.

In Latin, prevaricate means to 'walk crookedly' or 'deviate.'

If someone prevaricates, they often also procrastinate, which gives rise to confusion with the two words.

Overcome Procrastination

What we're going to be looking at in this book is how you can stop procrastinating and get back control of your life; not just now, but for the rest of your life.

Procrastination excels at one thing; making you feel bad. It's a power struggle that goes on in your mind and if you let procrastination win, not only will you suffer mentally and emotionally, but it will also ruin your life.

This is why it's imperative to stop wasting time and start living up to your full potential. This will not only have a positive impact on your physical and mental health, but it will help improve the life of those around you. It's win-win all the way and in everything you do.

14

So how do you begin?

You start by not procrastinating. Quit stalling on things you need to do. It sounds simple and it is because all you need to do is take the first step, and all the others will follow on naturally.

You see, procrastination is all in your mind. There's nothing physically holding you back from anything. It's just all in your mind. Every time you're not doing what you should be doing, it's because you don't want to start.

Starting something is always the hardest, yet surprisingly simple, part of doing anything. Once you take that first step and start, it's easier to keep going. Yet every day you have to overcome the resistance to starting.

Starting any project soon leads to feeling motivated to keep going, because once we've invested our time in something, even if it's only a few minutes, we don't want to stop and waste our investment.

The motivation you feel to keep going once you start leads to enjoying the process, which leads to achievement, money, satisfaction, education, no more stress over inaction, a better life, and accomplishment.

Once you've finished what you needed to do, it also leads to looking at others who've done it (or do it) too and see how they do it for more and better ideas so that you can improve and do more.

Starting something that you've been putting off, guarantees a feeling of achievement, even if you only commit to doing something for 30 minutes a day, it's still better than doing nothing at all.

A lot of people think that to do something you don't want to do (or can't be bothered to do) takes strong willpower or brute force, or a forced routine. But it takes none of that.

What you need is a commitment to change, a new mindset that you're going to start doing whatever needs to be done. No excuses. You'll do it no matter what. But you must WANT to change.

You just need to make a small start, even if it's huge project just doing one little thing makes all the difference.

Next you need to keep going, no matter what else comes up to try and distract you.

Finally, you must finish what you start.

Start something. Even if you only commit to doing it for 2 minutes, do it. (Put down your phone)

Keep going. Don't give up after the first blush. Keep starting again every day.

Finish it. See it through to the end. Finish your task. If something comes up, see to it, then get back to your task and finish it. This is mindset and commitment.

How to Start Right Now

Like I already said, overcoming procrastination and gaining control of your life takes your honest commitment to change. Don't just say you hope that what you're about to learn will make you feel committed to change, you have to already want to change.

You need to be ready to overcome your fear of doing things you need to do and be determined to do them.

You may have previously read books about overcoming procrastination that didn't help you. But this book is different because I'm going to tell you the exact steps you need to take. But then you must do them.

Reading this book won't help you unless you put what you learn into action. No one can do it for you. I'm going to help you by telling you what you need to do, but the rest is up to you.

What I can tell you, from my own experience, is that once you stop procrastinating and start taking action, the gratification is instant. Just making a start, no matter how small, will feel good.

But nothing will happen until you begin. Then once you begin, if you struggle and think you're going wrong with whatever you're doing, keep going. Don't use it as an excuse to give up. You'll figure things out as you go along.

Keep in mind that you're not aiming at perfection. Good enough is good enough. Just do the best you can do.

They say that on average, people procrastinate for 3 hours a day, which adds up to 45 days a year. That's a month and a half of doing absolutely nothing.

Just think, when you conquer procrastination you'll gain an extra 45 days a year that you can use for education, holidays, hobbies, a side business, house renovations/decorating, or creating a fabulous garden. Or do whatever you want to do.

Can you imagine having an extra 45 days every year to do whatever you want?

Now that's what I call taking back your life.

So to do that, let's get down to the nitty-gritty of why you procrastinate so much (3 hours a day), and how to stop.

3 Keys to Taking Back Control

Helplessness is one of the worst feelings that comes from procrastination. Being unable to get anything done because procrastination is holding you back, can even make you feel completely helpless.

But it doesn't have to be that way ever again. Control of your life is in your hands. It always was and always will be.

Once you're back in control you'll be an unstoppable productivity machine.

Not only will you get more done in a day than you ever imagined, but like all productive people, you'll be happy and content.

Right now though, you're probably hiding from others because you don't want to admit failure. You don't even want to admit it to yourself either. I'll bet you've thought up dozens of excuses as to why you never get anything done, and not one of them will be the real reason, which is that you're afraid to start. Scared of what? You're probably not even sure.

Do you get up every day, eager to get out of bed, thinking about all the things you're going to do, then spend the day doing very little, and go to bed wondering why you even bothered?

The good news is that it doesn't have to be that way. Not at all.

We're going to look at everything that's holding you back and what's making you so hesitant to start anything. Then we're going to look at how simple it is to turn your life around right now and feel good every day because you're living a happy and productive life.

And you start by getting one thing done which naturally flows on to doing more which feels like you get more hours out of every day.

Discovering why you procrastinate and putting an end to it starts right now.

What Makes You Procrastinate?

Before you can even begin to stop procrastinating, you first need to look at why you do it. Once you know why, it's easy to recognise yourself doing it, whereas right now you can't see it. Reading this book may even be a way you're procrastinating instead of doing what you're supposed to be doing right now.

So, we're going to look at 3 things.

1. **The root cause.**

   Why do you procrastinate?

   What things do you procrastinate about?

   What are you afraid of?

2. **What are your procrastination triggers?**

   At what point do you stop what you're doing?

   Or why don't you start?

   Are your triggers environmental or phycological?

3. **How can you take Control?**

   How do you make yourself do what needs to be done?

   At what point do you usually stop procrastinating and start doing?

   What needs to change?

You've probably not given much thought to why or how you procrastinate. In his book, *The War of Art,* Steven Pressfield calls it 'Resistance' (always spelled with a capital R) and says if we don't overcome it, it will ruin our lives. He speaks of Resistance as almost a living thing, an enemy to be conquered.

The problem with defeating procrastination, or Resistance, is that we usually lose because it's easier to do nothing than to start something. Also, once we habitually do something, including procrastinating, it's easy to keep doing what

19

we're doing. In fact, it's easy to procrastinate about stopping procrastinating (How ironic is that?).

All you need to do right now is take the first step, but first you need to figure out what that first step is.

It begins with not accepting your own excuses anymore.

Read this book, follow the steps, and procrastination will be banished for good. But ONLY if you do the work.

Remember, reading won't help you, but action will.

Understanding the root cause, recognizing your procrastination triggers, and talking back control, will make you feel powerful and give you back the confidence to know that you can tackle anything, no matter what.

Even if it's starting a project that you've never done before, you'll have the confidence to start and carry on, pushing through mistakes and seeing it through to the end.

You'll stop giving yourself excuses.

When something makes us feel good, when we stop procrastinating and start doing, it makes us want to do it again, which makes everything simpler and easier.

The Root Cause of Procrastination.

To overcome a problem, you first need to know what causes it.

- Why am I broke? Because I keep wasting money.
- Why am I miserable? Because I hate my job.
- Why am I always ill? Because my diet is unhealthy.
- Why does my back hurt? Because my mattress is saggy.

Knowing the root cause of a problem helps us overcome it, because we can see it clearly. This is knowledge, and knowledge is power.

With the clarity that knowledge gives you, you can achieve just about anything you set your mind to.

If you want something, go after it. It's that simple.

Once you understand the root cause of your procrastination, nothing can hold you back ever again.

Most people wallow in their own misery of never achieving anything. They never live up to their potential, but you'll be one of the elite few who does.

In fact, once you stop letting procrastination hold you back, you'll probably find that you're capable of achieving much more than you ever dreamed.

The great news is that with each achievement, you'll grow stronger.

Gaining satisfaction from whatever you do, not only makes you mentally stronger, but it also improves your life in so many ways.

Beat procrastination once, and you can do it again and again.

But how to beat it in the first place?

People think that to beat procrastination you need will power and discipline. While these two things may get you going, they won't help you carry through.

People also think that procrastination is simply laziness. But it's not. Just because you're not doing what you should be doing, doesn't mean you're doing nothing. You're still doing other things, just not the thing you're procrastinating about.

So what is it? What is procrastination?

Put simply, it's an avoidance tactic. And despite popular belief, it's not an unconscious habit. It's done consciously. We know we're doing it and are completely aware of our behaviour.

So, what are we avoiding?

We're avoiding what we're afraid of, which is criticism, failure, or starting.

Which one we're afraid of, and the tactics we use, depends on our personality type. We'll be looking at these in the next chapter, and you will recognise yourself as one of them. You'll know then, who you are, what it is you're afraid of, your triggers, and the avoidance tactics you use.

This will enable you to get more done. You'll find it easy to start anything AND keep going till you see it through to the end.

And THAT is success. Getting more done than you ever did before, every day. Plus, you'll have more time for other things too.

Days tend to go on as they start. So, start them right.

Different Procrastination Personalities.

We're now going to look at the different types of personalities when it comes to procrastination.

As I said previously, knowing what personality type you are, and the avoidance tactics you use, will enable you to get to the root cause of your procrastination.

So, let's take a look now.

There are 5 different types of personality, and each procrastinates in their own sneaky way. I say 'sneaky' because we lie to ourselves about why we procrastinate. We never want to admit it's procrastination.

In the following list of the 5 personality types, you'll see your type. Once you see it you can't unsee it and you will recognise yourself in the description.

Keep in mind that you're not alone. You're not the only one of your type. There are millions of others, but you are the only one who can conquer it.

Know thyself.

Once you've seen your type, you'll recognise when you're doing it. You can stop behaving that way immediately - but only if you want to. And I believe that you want to otherwise you wouldn't be reading this.

An important thing to keep in mind (and it's REALLY important), is that doing what you're supposed to be doing takes just as much time as avoiding it.

You won't gain any time by procrastinating, but you will lose achievement, feel bad, and know that you're going to do the exact same thing tomorrow.

Instead, know that tomorrow is the day that you'll quit procrastinating for good.

Look at the following 5 personality types and know which one is you.

It may be that you fit more than just one, so know your avoidance habits not just your type

1. The Perfectionist

You avoid starting anything because it's never the perfect time. If you do start something you never finish it because it's not good enough. You're never satisfied with what you do and think everything "could be better."

2. The Dreamer

You make lots of plans but rarely take any action. You always have plenty of ideas and can easily dream up more. You think and daydream often of how great it will be when you action your plans. Sadly, you never fulfill your dreams.

3. The Self-Saboteur

You have plenty to do but you can think of reasons not to do any of it. You consistently doubt your own ability which puts you off starting anything. You can't take criticism, so you never take action. Instead, you waste time on things that you can't do wrong like checking emails, binge watching TV, and other avoidance behaviours.

4. The Crisis Junkie

You always start things but never finish, so you end up with multiple projects on the go. Whenever you do finish something it's always at the last minute. You're always running late and in a time crunch as you hop from one unfinished project to the next.

5. The Busy Bee

You're always doing something yet achieving very little. You do lots of small, quick, unimportant tasks, to avoid the larger, important ones. You will busy yourself doing other tasks to avoid what you should be doing.

And that's it. Those are the 5 procrastinating personality types.

Which one are you? Or did you recognise yourself in more than one type.

Now you know not only your personality type, but also the type of behaviours you use to avoid doing what you should be doing.

So, what now?

It's simple. Now you must start.

Just start.

Whatever it is (and it can be multiple things) that you've been avoiding, start doing it. You don't have to finish, but you must make a start.

If you've been avoiding household chores, start by putting a few things away, put some washing into the washing machine, clear the kitchen counter tops and wipe them, pull up 10 weeds in the garden, brush a few cobwebs off the house, take your kids to the swings, walk your dog, clean one window.

Whatever it is, just start something.

Set a time every day to work. Use a diary. List everything you need to do in a day. Include everything, even time to go to the Gym or any appointment times.

Every day will be different, so make a new list daily. At the end of the day, make a list for the next day.

Timing everything you do can help too.

Years agon, there was a copywriter called Eugene Schwartz. He worked from home, which, like many of us, he found hard to do.

So, each morning, he would make a cup of tea, sit down at his desk, and set a timer for 33.33 minutes. He then had to work till the timer sounded.

He had a rule that he didn't have to work if he didn't want to, but he couldn't do anything else either. So, he could drink his tea, stare out the window, but nothing else. He said that some days, no matter how reluctant he was to start working, eventually boredom would make him take out his work and start reading through it, and within minutes he was back in writing-mode.

At the end of the 33.33 minutes, he had to get up and go do something else for 5 minutes, that didn't involve reading, so that his eyes were more distanced focused.

He'd then sit down and set his timer again. He'd do this timed routine of 33.33 minutes working and a 5-minute break, 4-6 times and then he was finished for the day.

He said that having only short working times made him stay focused so that he could get plenty done, plus he found it easier to start when he knew he only had to do it for a short time.

If you work from home (like I do) and you find it difficult to sit down every day, try the Eugene Schwartz method of only working for half an hour at a time so that you'll feel less reluctant to start, plus it will make you keep working because you know you haven't got much time.

I find a timed burst of work to be revealing because it shows me just how much I can get done in just 30 minutes. The short break is also helpful because it refreshes the mind.

Setting a timer for other things works too, and it shows you that things don't take as long as you think they will. It's also easier to make a start when you know you only have to do it for a short while. You could organise your morning in half-hour stints and get more done than you ever thought you possibly could.

I did this a lot when my kids were little. Every morning was divided into different chunks of time that always coincided with their favourite mid-morning TV show, so that I could sit and have a quiet cup of coffee for 20 minutes while they were engrossed in their TV show.

My mornings were something like: -

6-6.30am	Breakfast
6.30-7.30am	Kids up and breakfast
7.30-8am	Dishes and make drinks
8.00-9am	Cleaning and washing
9.00-10am	Shopping
10-10.30am	TV and coffee
10.30-11.30am	Walk dog
11.30-12.30am	Lunch

I was extremely organised back then because having young children and keeping them entertained all day required a strict routine.

And I still live by a routine because it means not only do I get a lot done, but it's so easy knowing what I need to do and where I need to be. It requires a lot less thinking time than having no plans and getting up every day with no clue what I'm going to be doing.

Starting is still the most important thing to conquer and it's easy if you have a time limit plus other things you have to do.

Doing something every day is better than doing nothing. Never think that the goal in life should be to do as little as possible. It isn't. The goal in life should be to live your best life, and you can't do that if you're not living up to your potential.

Starting is always satisfying, even if you don't think it will be before you do it, doing something always has its own rewards, both physical and mental.

When you start, you'll also quickly discover that practice makes things easier, and starting becomes a habit. Habits are easy.

As soon as you stop procrastinating and start doing, it will feel good to make even small steps forward, and minor accomplishments will feel like a huge achievement.

Conquering procrastination and starting things that you've been putting off for a long time, possibly even years, is life changing. It will change your life for the better in ways you never thought of.

Procrastinating makes you feel bad. Even if you think that avoiding doing something is only on your mind in a small way, you're wrong.

Those little things that niggle at your mind, when it goes on too long, can really bring you down.

Just remember that productive people are happy people. They feel good for getting things done, and so will you.

Stop Your Time-Wasting

Right now, you're reading this because you want to overcome procrastination. I know this because you wouldn't be reading this otherwise.

So, you should be congratulated for taking the first step.

But reading this book isn't enough.

You need to take action.

You may even be reading this book as a type of procrastination. But whatever is going on in your mind, it's time to act.

In the last chapter we looked at the different procrastination personality types, so you already know which type you are, and the avoidance tactics you're using.

Now it's time to quit wasting time and start being a hard-working 'machine' capable of doing anything you put your mind to.

It's time to let go of what's holding you back, and it starts with knowing your procrastination triggers and working through them.

Let's go through the 5 personality types, the reason you procrastinate, AND what to do about it.

The Perfectionist

You're afraid to finish what you start because you think nothing is ever good enough.

What you must do:

You must start and keep going, no matter what. Ignore the negative voice in your head telling you that what you're doing is bad. Finish everything you start. Stop giving yourself excuses to quit. Nothing will ever be perfect because it cannot be.

Let go of your ego and finish the task you've set for yourself.

Don't let your obsession with details take up all your time.

Be clear about why you're doing each of your tasks and assign a time limit to each. This will force you to stay focused and finish your task within the time frame.

For example, if you're going to write a report, be clear about why you're writing it. What is its purpose? What is the expected outcome of writing the report?

Being sure of why you're doing something, ensures that you don't waste time on small details that don't help you achieve your goal.

The Dreamer

You're afraid that nothing will ever be as good as you want it to be, so you're always stuck in the planning stage. You have too many plans yet not action.

What you must do:

Action each plan as soon as you finish writing it while your motivation is high.

Don't stop or make excuses. The expression "strike while the iron is hot" is extremely relevant for you because as soon as your motivation wanes, so does your action, so you find it easier to plan something else. Working your plan while you're highly motivated to do it, also makes your work great.

Stop being carried away by your endless imagination. Get your feet back on the ground by setting specific (and achievable) goals for each day.

Set a goal and break down the plan into small tasks that you can act on right away.

For example, if you want to get up earlier every day, set an actionable goal for it.

Then, break it down into smaller tasks:

- Every night I'll go to bed before 10pm.
- I'll set the alarm for 6am every day, even weekends.
- I won't plan any evening social events for the first month.
- When the alarm goes off, I'll get out of bed immediately.

Whatever your goal is, track your progress each day to see where you're going wrong and where to make changes. If your goal is large, monitor what you're spending your time on to see which tasks are a waste of time with little importance. This can help you focus on doing the things that bring positive results, and improve productivity.

The Self-Saboteur

You're afraid of people seeing you as a failure. You're afraid to do things in case they turn out "good enough" or "just ok."

What you must do:

Stop using avoidance tactics. Emails and social media are unimportant, and they steal your so much of your time and mental energy before you even notice. Don't start your days with these things.

Spend your mornings working on what you find the most challenging. This will help you build momentum for a productive day ahead, knowing that the most difficult tasks are already done.

Break down your tasks into smaller sub-tasks and list them in order of importance. Remember to be realistic about how much time each one will take.

Then do each task in order, one at a time, and only concentrating on the one you're doing.

Remember that if you do your best in everything you do, then everything will turn out the best it can.

No one is perfect. If your work turns out different to someone else's, it's just that; different. It's not better or worse, so don't compare or compete.

You don't have to be better than anyone else, just outwork them.

Writers know that someone who writes and publishes 20 "good enough" books, will attract more readers and make more sales that someone else who, at the same time, writes and publishes 2 or 3 "perfect" books.

It's the same with anything you do. Keep working and you'll always come out ahead.

The Crisis Junkie

You're afraid of not having enough time so you waste your time on unimportant tasks.

What you must do:

Stop believing that if you leave things to the last minute, rushing through them will make you perform better. It won't.

Stop rushing. Slow down.

Don't waste your time on unimportant tasks. When you know you have work to do, do it.

Buddhists say that the way to make more progress is to slow down and move 30% slower. This forces you to pay more attention to what you're doing and gives you the time you need to do what you need to do without making many mistakes. It also gives you more time to think about what you're doing.

You must understand that every move forward is a step further in the right direction. You'll never have enough time if you never start anything important.

Our work expands to fill the time we give ourselves to do it, so don't give yourself more time than you need, or you'll dilly-dally and waste time.

Don't worry about time. Just start and see how far you get. Not starting is the biggest waste of time. The longer you procrastinate and don't start, the longer things will take.

Why sit and worry when you could be starting?

The Busy Bee

You waste time on unimportant tasks because you're afraid of putting in a lot of effort on the big, important things.

What you must do:

You must get your priorities straight.

Before you do anything, look at what it is that you're about to spend your time on and ask yourself, what is the purpose of doing this? What is the expected outcome?

Important tasks should take priority over urgent ones because "urgent" doesn't always mean important. You only have so much time and energy, so don't waste that on things that don't matter.

Important tasks are the ones that add value in the long run.

For example, replying to an email that says, "please respond promptly" seems urgent, but before you reply to that email, think about how important it is compared to other tasks. Just make a note to answer it later and get back to doing what's more important.

If a project looks big and overwhelming, break it down into smaller tasks.

Then do them one at a time. When you finish one task, start the next task on the list.

Tick off each one as you do it so that your progress feels faster.

Effort is never wasted.

Now you know what it takes to overcome each of the avoidance tactics of each procrastinating personality type.

Whatever it is that you want to do, don't think about the outcome. Just concentrate on each task to be done. Do everything one job at a time.

You don't have a whole garden to weed, you just need to spend an hour a day in the garden pulling up one weed at a time.

You don't have a whole meal to make, just some potatoes and vegetables to prepare for later.

You don't have a whole novel to write, you only have one character to create and a difficult situation to put them in.

Whatever it is that you have to do, think of the first thing you need to do, then go do that.

Keeping things simple makes them feel less daunting.

Remember that starting is always the hardest part, so once you start, it gets easier from there. The more things you start, the more invincible you'll feel.

No one likes a quitter, not even you, so stop being one. Stop letting yourself down.

Know who you are and see how much you're capable of doing every day.

You'll find that you can accomplish more in one week than you usually do in a month.

The Evil of Social Media

If you let it, social media can become your nemesis, the thing that takes over your life and destroys it. Not only can it suck the life out of your life, but it can cause mental depression and a feeling of despair and hopelessness.

My advice to everyone is to stay the hell away from social media. It can waste hours of your time and leave you feeling anxious and helpless.

What you need is a complete digital detox. Don't just minimize your time spent on social media, have a complete break.

Just try it for one week. Don't check any social media sites and don't look at your phone when you're walking. When you're waiting at a bus stop, or in a queue somewhere, refrain from taking out your phone. Instead, look around you and become familiar with your surroundings, or use the time to breathe deeply and quiet your mind and body. You won't realize how much social media has taken over your life until you stop letting it.

Imagine how great it would be to start each day without looking at a screen. The alarm goes off, you get straight out of bed and begin your day with no phone in sight. You have breakfast, do a few chores, go to work, come home, have dinner, work on a side-hustle, watch TV, then go to bed and sleep well, because you feel so productive.

Instead of staring at your phone for several hours a day, you use the time to work your side-hustle so that you can quit your job and have financial independence.

You'd have time to do everything. A clean home, time with your kids, time with your spouse, home-cooked meals, a home business, a well-kept garden, and a clean car. You can have all these things if you practice digital minimalism.

Don't believe me?

Look at it this way; the average person spends 4 hours a day looking at their phone (or another screen). And if that's just the average, it means that many spend way more than 4 hours a day staring at their phone.

Every day I see people staring at their phones while they walk down the street, push their kids on the swings, shop in the supermarket, drive their car, and while they cross a busy road.

I often see couples who are ignoring each other because they're both engrossed in whatever they're looking at on their phones.

And it's not just social media that is taking up most of their daily attention. They're also surfing online going from one pointless blog post to the next, scrolling through forums looking for others whose opinions match theirs, or sending or receiving pointless text messages.

So, consider this, everything online is marketing. Websites exist to make money. They want you on their site so that they can make money from you directly or from the advertisers on their site.

Social media sites do everything they can to keep you there because the longer you're there, the more money they make. Many online advertisements earn money from how many views they get. This means that you don't have to click on an advertisement for the site owner to make money, it just must be visible on the page you're looking at.

This is why social media sites want you to stay as long as possible and click 'like' on many things. Once they know what you 'like' then they know what type of ads to show you. And the more ads they show you, the more money they make. It's all about the marketing.

We're all led to believe that social media is all about being 'social,' a way to keep up with friends and family. But it's not, and it's not what people use it for. It's a place where people give their opinions and others attack them and tell them how wrong they are.

People treat others much worse online than they ever do in person. This is what makes it a terrible place to spend time.

We all know that social media has caused some people to commit suicide because of the appalling comments hurled at them online. Yet still these sites go on encouraging people to stay for hours, to 'follow' more people, to click everything they 'like' and give their biased opinion to strangers.

There's a saying that you should never waste time arguing with an idiot on social media. How do you know they're an idiot? Because they're arguing with an idiot on social media.

Online games are another thing that can lower your mood and take hours out of your day. Some people get so obsessed with online gaming that they become addicted and will let go of their job and their spouse, just so they can carry on playing.

Yet all these things have no purpose. They are completely pointless. Whether you're spending your time on games, social media, email, or reading blogs, don't think that it's all about you.

It's not. It's all about marketing. It's about companies looking for gullible procrastinators; people who want to waste their life staring at a screen as an avoidance tactic, to avoid doing what they should be doing.

Don't let them steal your life any longer.

I once did a digital detox for a week. I deleted most of the apps on my phone, stayed off social media completely, and unsubscribed from nearly all the newsletters in my email list. I also never have notifications turned on for email or social media, or I would have turned them off too. For a week I only responded to text messages that required an immediate response.

What happened that week was that I gained so much more time every day. I bounded out of bed and got on with my day without checking my emails or picking up my phone. I also quickly discovered that when you stop responding to unnecessary text messages, people stop sending them, which is so freeing.

I got so much more done that week, and I had more of my attention to give to those I was interacting with. I'm not even a heavy user of social media and I don't use my phone a lot, yet doing a one-week digital detox felt like I was living in a whole new world.

But because I work online, I still needed to check my email and upload posts to social media. So, I decided to minimize the time to do it and I did it in 2 batches. I checked my email only twice that week and posted to social media just once. I also timed both sessions so that it didn't take more than 30 minutes, and I scheduled the social media posts so that I didn't need to keep logging in every day to post them all separately.

After that week, I felt so happy spending time off-line, that I've never gone back.

"Offline is the new peace of mind."

~ Mind Mastery

I used to check my emails and social media accounts every morning. Now I check them in the afternoon when I've finished for the day, and I don't check them every day.

Try it yourself for a week. Delete apps from your phone, turn off notifications, don't check email, stay off social media, and don't respond to unnecessary texts.

Instead look up and experience life instead of always looking down at your phone. Also, remove the auto sign-in of your accounts so that your less tempted to check them. During your downtime do something different like read, walk, do chores, listen to podcasts or audio books. I usually listen to something while I'm doing chores. It makes me want to do them so that I can carry on listening.

If you want to know how much time you're wasting online, there are apps you can download that measure how much time you use your phone. There are also apps that can block you from using your phone at certain times of the day, or can block you from using certain apps/websites at certain times.

Do whatever it takes for you to spend less time online.

Don't use your phone in bed and stop reaching for it as soon as you wake up every morning.

And never, ever, look at your phone when you're walking or driving.

It's time to take back control of your life. Stop letting social media sites and bloggers steal your time.

Remember, social media is NOT social. It's just a way for marketers to make money out of you. Don't click 'like.' Never forget that they're watching everything you do to figure out how gullible you are.

Not only that, but my own experience tells me that people who spend a lot of time on social media are awful people. They spend their time trolling others in the comments or posting hundreds of photos of a fake and deliriously happy life that they want people to believe. Either way, they are best avoided.

Try a one-week digital detox, even if you think it won't make a difference, try it anyway. Then keep cutting down on your screen time until it becomes a minimal part of your day.

At first, digital freedom seems unnatural because staring at a screen has become so entrenched in our lives that it feels natural. We're even afraid to leave the house without our phones.

Digital freedom will make you feel better about yourself than you have in years.

Spending too much time online is like banging your head repeatedly against a wall.

You don't realize how much it's hurting you until you stop.

End Procrastination and Take Back Control

Now we've come to the end of this book, so it's time for you to end procrastination for good and take back control of your life.

But you can't take back control until you know how. You need a plan.

You need a plan to get your life to how you want it. You already know the life you want. In your mind you know what you want to do. What you want in your life are the things that you procrastinate about.

So, because you already know what you want, it's time to stop dreaming and start doing.

Procrastination feels bad.

Productivity feels good.

"I feel awful about how much I got done today," said nobody, ever.

All it takes is for you to start. Take the first step, whatever that is for you, and it will be easy to keep going.

The first step might be deleting online accounts, unfollowing, unsubscribing, putting your phone in a drawer, writing in your journal, getting up on the alarm every morning, clearing clutter, buying healthy food, going for a walk, cleaning out the car, taking your kids to the park, signing up for a course, starting the novel you've always wanted to write, or something as simple as picking up your dirty clothes and putting them in the laundry hamper.

And never procrastinate again.

Don't make the mistake of becoming bogged down in unnecessary tasks. Know what your goal is, what you want to accomplish, and then work towards getting it done.

Here are 3 things that you need to keep in mind.

1. Know your goals

This seems simple, but it requires a bit of thought. You need to understand what it is that you want to do so that you don't waste time on unnecessary things.

With everything you want to do, you need to separate needs from wants, the important things from the unnecessary things.

Each goal will have 3 things: -

1. **Must haves.** These are essential things you need to do to reach your goal.

2. **Should haves.** These are important, but not immediately essential. Things that you could do later.

3. **Could haves.** Also known as 'good to haves.' These things are nice, but not necessary. They can be left out if must haves and should haves turn out to be longer than expected.

Let me explain this more.

The above things are a matter of balancing your priorities with every goal, no matter how small or large that goal is.

As an example, say your goal is to wash your car.

You must clean it inside and out.

You should have the proper equipment, but rags and a hose will do if that's all you've got.

You could wax it too, but it's not necessary, it's too time consuming, and the car is still clean without it.

If you're having a baby and don't know what you need

You must have baby clothes, a car seat, and a pram.

You should have a cot, but the pram will be enough to start with.

You could splash out on all the latest baby gadgets, but they are unnecessary, and you can better judge what you need as you go along.

If you want to set up a blog.

You must have a domain name and hosting.

You should have a few affiliate products to offer so that you can make money, but they're not necessary yet.

You could have a unique, custom-made blog designed for you, but the content is more important right now.

2. Limit Your Time

They say that our work expands to fill the time we give it, so don't give it too much time or it won't get done.

If you give yourself 3 weeks to do a job that you think will only take 1 week, you'll delay doing it, and may get bored and never do it at all.

It's so much better to set a short time to get something done and then challenge yourself.

When the time is up, stop. Why? Because knowing that you have to stop makes you work faster.

You can limit your time by saying that you must finish a task by lunchtime, or that you can't have lunch until you finish it. That will make you get up earlier.

Use a phone blocker if you need to. Do whatever it takes to get your work done.

Use time blocks. Divide your morning into blocks of time. Set a timer and monitor how much you can get done in each block.

If you don't finish a task in the allotted time, finish it later. But make sure you do it.

Never end a day with tasks unfinished.

3. Reduce Your Tasks

This makes reaching your goals so easy.

Break your goal down into individual tasks.

Set a time to complete each task.

Knowing all the steps involved, and the order to do them in makes it clear to see what you need to do, how to do it, when to do it, and when to begin.

You can even see if you need to begin earlier.

As an example, take the goal of cleaning your car. It sounds simple, but if you're standing there, looking at your car with no idea how you're going to do it, or where to start, then you'll be reluctant to start at all.

It simplifies it if you write down each task, as follows:

Clean Outside - Hose, wipe down, clean wheels.

Inside - empty everything out

take out mats

vacuum inside (seats, floor, and boot)

vacuum mats

polish inside doors and dash

put back mats and necessary items

throw rubbish in bin

take other stuff inside

With that list you know you need a hose, cleaning cloths, rubbish bag, polish, duster, vacuum cleaner. You also know that you'll begin with the hose, so that makes it easy to start.

You could also allot time to the different tasks to see how long it takes to do each one and how long it will take altogether.

I always start projects as early as possible just in case something takes longer than I thought, especially when it comes to jobs like cleaning the car because once you start you have no option but to finish.

Knowing how long it takes to do things helps with planning and stops procrastination because you know how much time it will take to complete a project.

You can set a timer for each task and compete against the clock to get things done.

Be strong about what you're doing. Don't let anyone or anything distract you. Have a determined mindset and you won't go wrong.

Start projects as early as possible so that if other things come up, at least you get the important tasks finished.

I always find that when I'm working on a big project, or even a small but important one, the universe throws up all sorts of distractions in my way so that I feel like I'm always jumping hurdles.

You may have noticed this phenomenon yourself.

If you're driving somewhere, and you're not in a rush and have plenty of time to get there, you'll get every green traffic-light and no traffic congestion. But if you set off late, every light will be red and there'll be roadworks and other hold ups along the way.

One day, I was rushing because I had to go out for a few hours, and I had to catch the bus. I had a few errands to run first plus I wanted to walk my dog before I left.

I managed to get everything done, but only had 30 minutes to walk my dog, who was a greyhound. I quickly clipped his lead to his collar and said, 'let's go' as we set off for his walk.

We lived in a small, chatty town at that time so I swore to myself that no matter who I ran into, I wouldn't stop to chat because I didn't have a minute to spare.

As I walked, I tried to keep my head down so that no one could catch my eye. I was determined to stop for no one.

I got as far as nearly the end of the walk and was just about to round the last corner when a friendly voice said, 'Oh what a beautiful dog."

I turned and was about to say, 'thanks,' and rush off, but I couldn't.

When I turned towards the voice, it was a smiling Buddhist nun dressed in a crimson robe. She looked so happy to see my dog and she said, 'May I pat him?'

My greyhound, hearing a friendly voice, turned to her and wagged his tail. The nun instantly stroked his head and began to tell him how gorgeous he was and how fortunate she was to meet him.

I was stunned. The universe had challenged me. I'd said that there was no one, not anyone, that I was going to stop for. It hadn't crossed my mind that I'd run into a Buddhist nun. It had never happened before and has never happened since. But that one day at that one time, we crossed paths. And she was probably the one person I could never say no to. I have a lot of respect for Buddhist monks and nuns.

So, there I stood for a few minutes, chatting to the smiling nun (she was a lovely person) while she asked me about my dog and told me how much she missed having pets. And then I had to get home quick and get ready because if I missed my bus it was 2 hours till the next one. I made it with seconds to spare. And funnily enough, when I walked back towards the bus stop, the nun was nowhere in sight.

But this is how things always happen. When you have a determined mindset, life will throw a multitude of distractions at you.

That's how you know you're doing the right thing. It's like a test to see how true you are to your principles, to see if you really are strong enough and determined enough to do what you say you're going to do.

Life will throw stumbling blocks at you all the time. Don't ever think it won't. Just don't let these things stop you. Things that come up may delay your progress, but nothing will stop you unless you let it.

Don't let it.

It's your life and you need to live it to your full potential in all areas. It doesn't matter if you're doing household chores, looking after your children, studying for a degree, writing a book, building a house, knitting some socks, setting up your own business, walking your dog, having a day out with family, or making a cake.

44

Whatever you're doing and everything you do, do it the best you can. Do everything to the best of your ability.

Don't cheat yourself by doing things badly, or worse, not doing them at all.

Even worse than that, don't do anything that will hurt you or hurt someone else.

Just imagine how great it would be if you did everything you wanted to do in life. All those things that were listed earlier (studying for a degree, spending time with your kids, setting up your own business, etc.) imagine if you were doing all of them. I know that might sound extreme and you may think it would be impossible to do all those things, but what if I told you it's not?

Can you, the great procrastinator, feel what it would be like to do everything you've ever wanted to do in life? And as I said, it doesn't have to be life-altering things.

That's the beauty of not procrastinating. It's all the little things that you do that adds up to a huge change in life.

You can save up for your dream home, start a hobby, get a degree or other form of further education, have a clean and tidy house, write that novel you've always wanted to write, and a whole lot more.

And the best thing about making a start and getting things done, is that it then becomes easier to go on and do so much more.

That feeling of being back in control of your life is priceless.

You'll have the confidence to say no to things you don't want, and the courage to say no to the people who try and hold you back. And they will.

One of the downsides of being in control of your life and moving forward, is that no one will want you to succeed, especially if they themselves are failing. They also won't like that you've become too busy to waste time with them.

Sadly, you'll find that your own family will try and stop you. They won't feel comfortable if you become a different person.

And you will.

When you stop procrastinating and start getting things done and start moving on with your life, you'll become a different person, a more positive person, and those closest to you won't want you to change.

They feel comfortable with the procrastinator that you usually are, that person stagnating in life, doing nothing, and going nowhere.

But once you get up out of your chair with your new mindset and determination to procrastinate no more, you're going to make others uncomfortable.

If you're prepared for that, then they won't hold you back, because you won't let them.

Listening to nay-sayers is just another form of procrastination.

So now it's time for you to stop reading and start doing and walk into your new life.

You already know what it is that you want in life, and I don't mean just the one major thing.

There will be one major thing that you want to do with your life, but there are also lots of little things too, including those seemingly unimportant things that niggle at your unconscious every day.

You probably ignore all the things you want in life because up until now, it's been easier to let procrastination steal your dreams.

But you can't ignore them anymore because you now know how easy it is to beat procrastination.

All you have to do is start. Begin the first task you need to do to move you towards your goals.

Start with one of your smaller goals if it helps. Or go big and go for what you really want.

It really is up to you now.

Reading this book can only take you so far. Now it's time to stop reading and start doing.

And I wish you all the best in your new non-procrastinating life.

I know you'll enjoy taking back control.

End.

CPSIA information can be obtained
at www.ICGtesting.com
Printed in the USA
BVHW071848151222
654336BV00012B/902

9 780645 450262